EASY POP MELODIES

FOR TRUMPET

ISBN 978-1-4803-8432-3

HAL•LEONARD® CORPORATION

7777 W. BLUEMOUND RD. P.O. BOX 13819 MILWAUKEE, WI 53213

Visit Hal Leonard Online at
www.halleonard.com

ALL MY LOVING

TRUMPET

Words and Music by JOHN LENNON
and PAUL McCARTNEY

BEAUTY AND THE BEAST

from Walt Disney's BEAUTY AND THE BEAST

TRUMPET

Lyrics by HOWARD ASHMAN
Music by ALAN MENKEN

BLOWIN' IN THE WIND

TRUMPET

Words and Music by
BOB DYLAN

CAN YOU FEEL THE LOVE TONIGHT

from Walt Disney Pictures' THE LION KING

TRUMPET

Music by ELTON JOHN
Lyrics by TIM RICE

CAN'T HELP FALLING IN LOVE

TRUMPET

Words and Music by GEORGE DAVID WEISS,
HUGO PERETTI and LUIGI CREATORE

CLOCKS

TRUMPET

Words and Music by GUY BERRYMAN,
JON BUCKLAND, WILL CHAMPION
and CHRIS MARTIN

DAYDREAM BELIEVER

TRUMPET

Words and Music by
JOHN STEWART

DON'T KNOW WHY

TRUMPET

Words and Music by
JESSE HARRIS

DON'T STOP BELIEVIN'

TRUMPET

Words and Music by STEVE PERRY,
NEAL SCHON and JONATHAN CAIN

EDELWEISS

from THE SOUND OF MUSIC

TRUMPET

Lyrics by OSCAR HAMMERSTEIN II
Music by RICHARD RODGERS

EIGHT DAYS A WEEK

TRUMPET

Words and Music by JOHN LENNON
and PAUL McCARTNEY

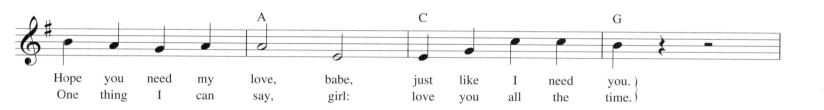

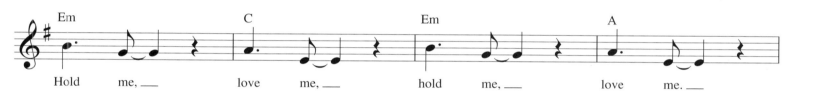

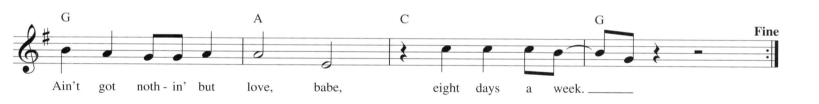

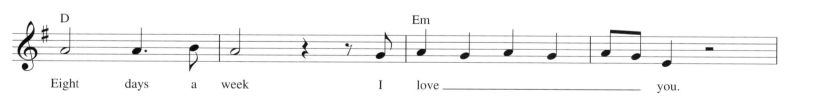

EVERY BREATH YOU TAKE

TRUMPET

Music and Lyrics by
STING

Ev - 'ry breath you __ take,　　ev - 'ry move you __ make,
Ev - 'ry move you __ make,　　ev - 'ry vow you __ break,

ev - 'ry bond you break, ev - 'ry step you take, I'll be watch - ing you.
ev - 'ry smile you fake, ev - 'ry claim you stake, I'll be watch - ing you.

Ev - 'ry sin - gle __ day,　　ev - 'ry word you __ say,

ev - 'ry game you play, ev - 'ry night you stay, I'll be watch-ing you.

Oh, can't you __ see　　you be - long to __ me?

How my poor heart __ aches __　　with ev - 'ry step __ you take.

FIREFLIES

TRUMPET

Words and Music by
ADAM YOUNG

GEORGIA ON MY MIND

Words by STUART GORRELL
Music by HOAGY CARMICHAEL

TRUMPET

IN MY LIFE

TRUMPET

Words and Music by JOHN LENNON
and PAUL McCARTNEY

HEY, SOUL SISTER

TRUMPET

Words and Music by PAT MONAHAN,
ESPEN LIND and AMUND BJORKLAND

Moderately

Hey, _____ hey, _____ hey. _____

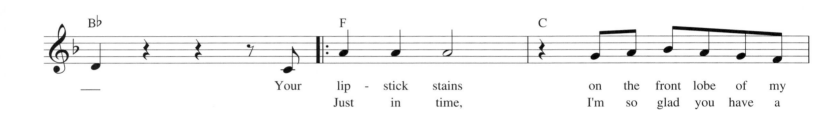

_____ Your lip - stick stains on the front lobe of my
Just in time, I'm so glad you have a

left - side brains. I know I wouldn't for - get ya, and so I went and
one - track mind like me. You gave my life di - rec - tion, a game show love con -

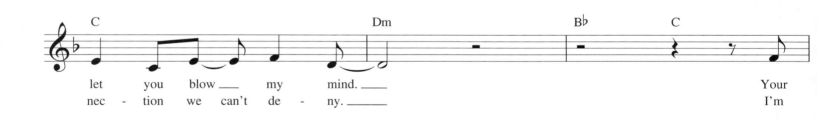

let you blow _____ my mind. _____ Your
nec - tion we can't de - ny. _____ I'm

sweet moon - beam, the smell of you in ev - 'ry sin - gle dream I dream. _____
so ob - sessed; my heart is bound to beat right out my un - trimmed chest. _____

I knew when we col - lid - ed you're the one I have de - cid - ed who's one of my kind. _

I be - lieve in you; like a vir - gin, you're Ma - don - na, and I'm al - ways gon - na

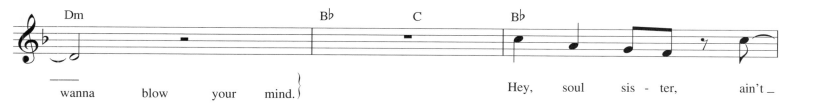

wanna blow your mind. Hey, soul sis - ter, ain't _

that Mis - ter Mis - ter on the ra - di - o, ster - e - o? The way you move ain't fair, you know.

Hey, soul sis - ter, I _____ don't wan - na miss a sin - gle thing you do _____

to - night. Hey, _____ hey, _____

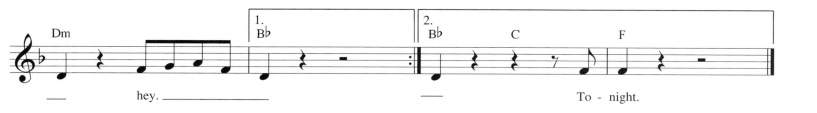

hey. _____ To - night.

HOT N COLD

TRUMPET

Words and Music by KATY PERRY,
MAX MARTIN and LUKASZ GOTTWALD

Moderately fast

You change your mind ___ like a girl ___ chang-es clothes. ___
We used to be ___ just like twins, ___ so in sync. ___

___ Yeah, you P - M - S ___ like a bitch; ___
___ The same en - er - gy ___ now's a dead ___

___ I would know. ___ And you o - ver - think, ___
___ bat - ter - y. ___ Used to laugh 'bout noth - ing; ___

___ al - ways speak ___ cryp - tic - 'ly. ___ I should know ___
___ now you're plain ___ bor - ing. ___ I should know ___

___ that you're ___ no good ___ for me. _____
___ that you're ___ not gon - na change. _____

'Cause you're hot ___ then you're cold. You're yes ___ then you're no. You're in ___

___ then you're out. You're up ___ then you're down. You're wrong ___ when it's right. It's black ___

___ and it's white. We fight, ___ we break up. We kiss, ___ we make up. ___

You don't real - ly wan - na stay, no, ___ but you don't real - ly wan - na

go. _____ You're hot ___ then you're cold. You're yes ___ then you're no. You're in ___

___ then you're out. You're up ___ then you're down. _ ___ then you're down. _

ISN'T SHE LOVELY

TRUMPET

Words and Music by
STEVIE WONDER

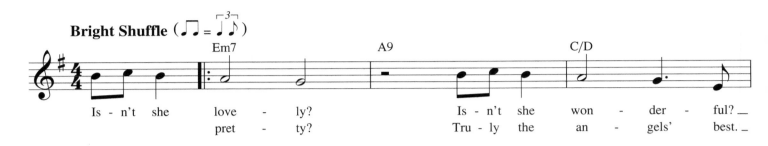

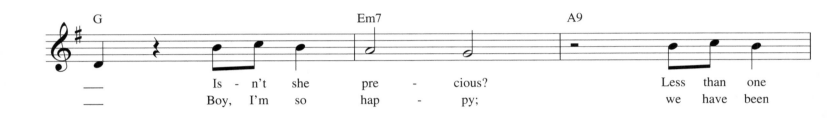

THE LETTER

TRUMPET

Words and Music by
WAYNE CARSON THOMPSON

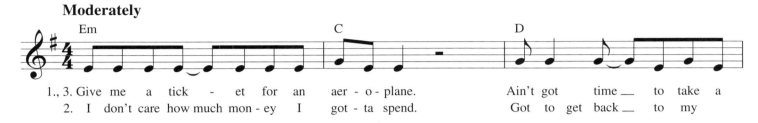

1., 3. Give me a tick - et for an aer - o - plane.　Ain't got time __ to take a
2. I don't care how much mon - ey I got - ta spend.　Got to get back __ to my

fast __ train. }　　Lone - ly days are gone; __　I'm a - go - in' home. __ Oh, my
ba - by again. }

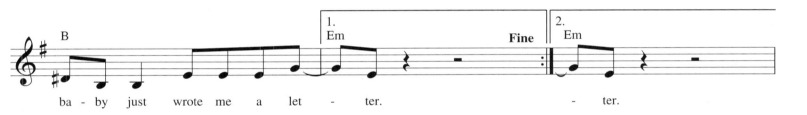

ba - by just wrote me a let - ter.　　　- ter.

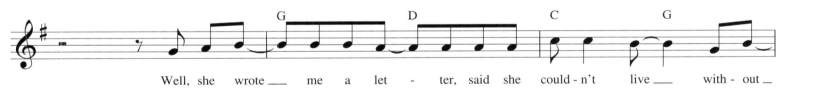

Well, she wrote __ me a let - ter, said she could - n't live __ with - out __

__ me no more.　　Lis - ten, mis - ter, can't you see I

D.C. al Fine
(take 1st ending)

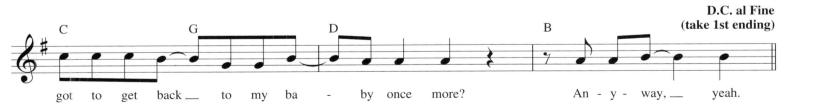

got to get back __ to my ba - by once more?　An - y - way, __ yeah.

LIKE A VIRGIN

TRUMPET

Words and Music by BILLY STEINBERG
and TOM KELLY

THE LOOK OF LOVE

from CASINO ROYALE

TRUMPET

Words by HAL DAVID
Music by BURT BACHARACH

LOVE ME TENDER

TRUMPET

Words and Music by ELVIS PRESLEY
and VERA MATSON

Moderately

Love me ten - der, love me sweet; nev - er let me
Love me ten - der, love me long; take me to your

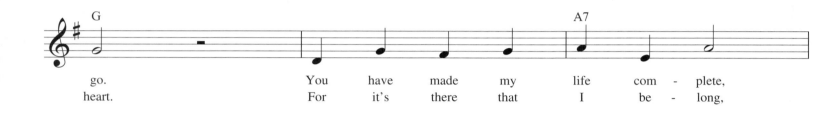

go. You have made my life com - plete,
heart. For it's there that I be - long,

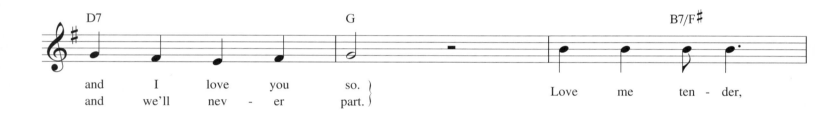

and I love you so. ⎫ Love me ten - der,
and we'll nev - er part. ⎭

love me true. All my dreams ful - fill.

For, my dar - ling, I love you, and I al - ways

will. and I al - ways will.

MR. TAMBOURINE MAN

TRUMPET

Words and Music by
BOB DYLAN

LOVE STORY

TRUMPET

Words and Music by
TAYLOR SWIFT

Moderately

We were both young when I first saw __ you. I close my eyes __ and the

flash-back starts. _ I'm stand-ing there on a bal-co-ny in sum-mer air.

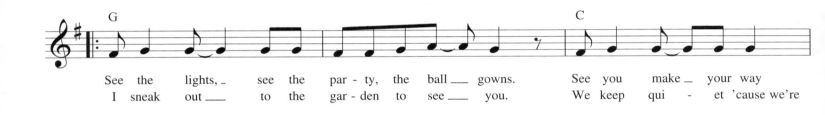

See the lights, _ see the par - ty, the ball __ gowns. See you make __ your way
I sneak out __ to the gar - den to see __ you. We keep qui - et 'cause we're

through the crowd_ and say hel - lo. Lit - tle did I _____ know
dead if they knew, _ so close your eyes, es - cape this town for a lit - tle while.

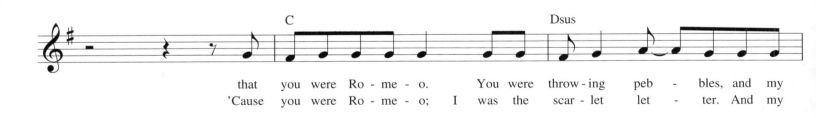

that you were Ro - me - o. You were throw - ing peb - bles, and my
'Cause you were Ro - me - o; I was the scar - let let - ter. And my

dad - dy said, "Stay a - way from Ju - li - et." __ And I was cry - ing on the stair - case,
dad - dy said, "Stay a - way from Ju - li - et." __ But you were ev - 'ry - thing to me. I was

beg - ging you, please, __ don't go. _____ And I _____ said:

Ro - me - o, take me some-where we can be a - lone. I'll be wait - ing.

All there's left to do is run. You'll be the prince and I'll be the prin - cess.

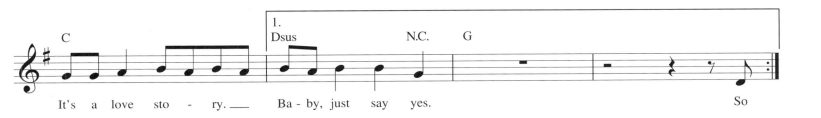

It's a love sto - ry. ___ Ba - by, just say yes. So

Ba - by, just say ___ yes. ___ Oh, ___ oh, oh. ___

Oh, ___ oh, oh, ___ oh.

'Cause we were both young when I first saw ___ you. ___

MOON RIVER

from the Paramount Picture BREAKFAST AT TIFFANY'S

Words by JOHNNY MERCER
Music by HENRY MANCINI

TRUMPET

MORNING HAS BROKEN

TRUMPET

Words by ELEANOR FARJEON
Music by CAT STEVENS

MY CHERIE AMOUR

TRUMPET

Words and Music by STEVIE WONDER,
SYLVIA MOY and HENRY COSBY

MY GIRL

TRUMPET

Words and Music by WILLIAM "SMOKEY" ROBINSON
and RONALD WHITE

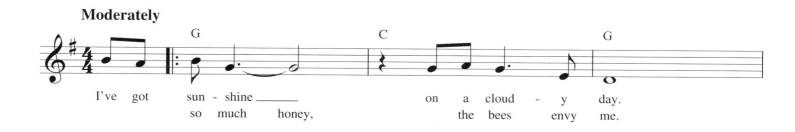

I've got sun - shine _____ on a cloud - y day.
so much honey, the bees envy me.

When it's cold out - side, I've got the month of
I've got a sweet - er song than the birds in the

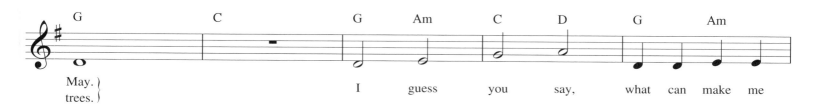

May. ⎫ I guess you say, what can make me
trees. ⎭

feel this way? My girl. (My girl, my girl.) Talk - in' 'bout

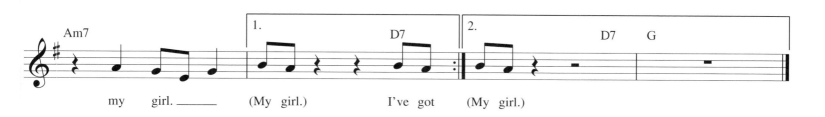

my girl. _____ (My girl.) I've got (My girl.)

MY FAVORITE THINGS
from THE SOUND OF MUSIC

TRUMPET

Lyrics by OSCAR HAMMERSTEIN II
Music by RICHARD RODGERS

Brightly

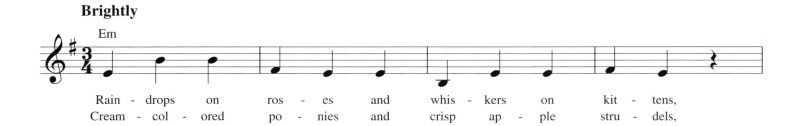

Rain - drops on ros - es and whis - kers on kit - tens,
Cream - col - ored po - nies and crisp ap - ple stru - dels,

bright cop - per ket - tles and warm wool - en mit - tens,
door - bells and sleigh - bells and schnit - zel with noo - dles,

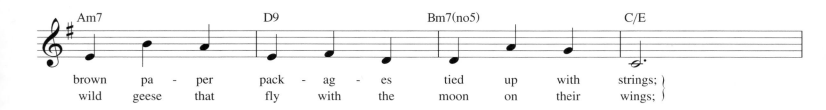

brown pa - per pack - ag - es tied up with strings;)
wild geese that fly with the moon on their wings;)

these are a few of my fa - vor - ite things.

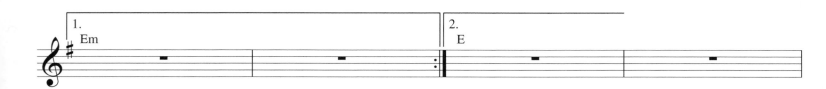

Girls in white dress - es with blue sat - in sash - es,

MY HEART WILL GO ON
(Love Theme from 'Titanic')
from the Paramount and Twentieth Century Fox Motion Picture TITANIC

Music by JAMES HORNER
Lyric by WILL JENNINGS

TRUMPET

NIGHTS IN WHITE SATIN

TRUMPET

Words and Music by
JUSTIN HAYWARD

NOWHERE MAN

TRUMPET

Words and Music by JOHN LENNON
and PAUL McCARTNEY

PUFF THE MAGIC DRAGON

TRUMPET

Words and Music by LENNY LIPTON
and PETER YARROW

RAINDROPS KEEP FALLIN' ON MY HEAD
from BUTCH CASSIDY AND THE SUNDANCE KID

TRUMPET

Lyric by HAL DAVID
Music by BURT BACHARACH

SCARBOROUGH FAIR/CANTICLE

TRUMPET

Arrangement and Original Counter Melody by PAUL SIMON
and ARTHUR GARFUNKEL

SOMEWHERE OUT THERE

from AN AMERICAN TAIL

TRUMPET

Music by BARRY MANN and JAMES HORNER
Lyric by CYNTHIA WEIL

Moderately

Some - where out there, be - neath the pale moon -

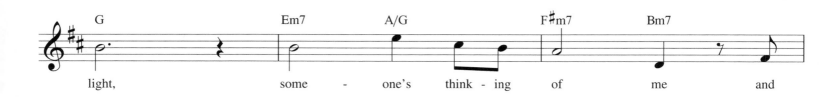

light, some - one's think - ing of me and

lov - ing me to - night. Some - where

out there, some - one's say - ing a prayer that

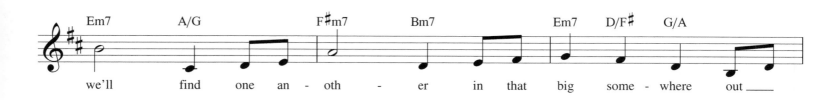

we'll find one an - oth - er in that big some - where out ____

there. And e - ven though I know how ver - y far a - part we are, it

helps to think we might be wish - ing on the same bright star. And

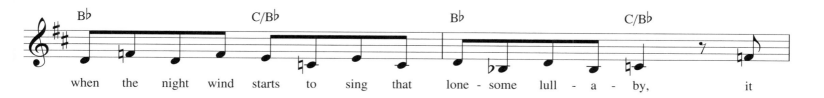

when the night wind starts to sing that lone - some lull - a - by, it

helps to think we're sleep - ing un - der - neath the same big sky.

Some - where out there, if love can see us

through, then we'll be to - geth - er some - where

out there, out where dreams come true.

THE SOUND OF MUSIC

from THE SOUND OF MUSIC

TRUMPET

Lyrics by OSCAR HAMMERSTEIN II
Music by RICHARD RODGERS

The hills are a-live with the sound of mu - sic, _____ with

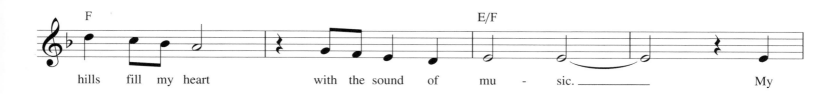

songs they have sung for a thou - sand years. _____ The

hills fill my heart with the sound of mu - sic. _____ My

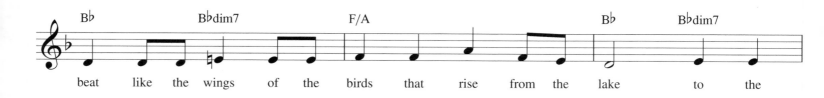

heart wants to sing ev - 'ry song it hears. _____ My heart wants to

beat like the wings of the birds that rise from the lake to the

trees. My heart wants to sigh like a chime that flies from a

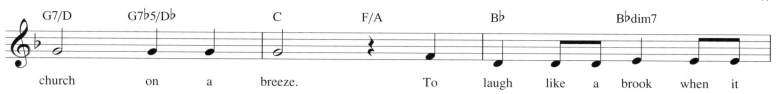

church on a breeze. To laugh like a brook when it

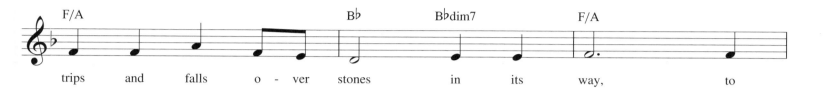

trips and falls o - ver stones in its way, to

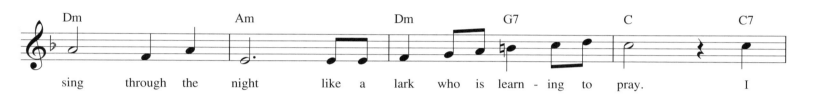

sing through the night like a lark who is learn - ing to pray. I

go to the hills when my heart is lone - ly. _____ I

know I will hear what I've heard be - fore. _____ My

heart will be blessed with the sound of mu - sic, _____ and I'll

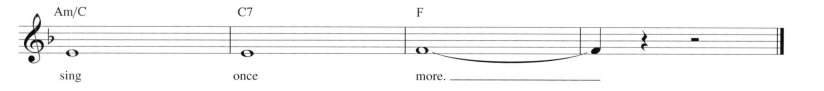

sing once more. _____

STRANGERS IN THE NIGHT
adapted from A MAN COULD GET KILLED

Words by CHARLES SINGLETON and EDDIE SNYDER
Music by BERT KAEMPFERT

TRUMPET

SUNSHINE ON MY SHOULDERS

TRUMPET

Words by JOHN DENVER
Music by JOHN DENVER, MIKE TAYLOR
and DICK KNISS

SWEET CAROLINE

TRUMPET

Words and Music by
NEIL DIAMOND

Moderately

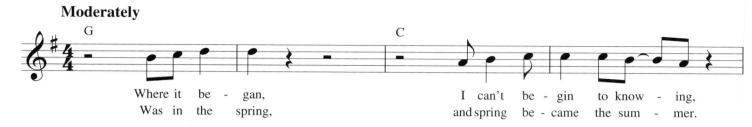

Where it be - gan,
Was in the spring,
I can't be - gin to know - ing,
and spring be - came the sum - mer.

but then, I know it's grow - ing strong.
Who'd have be - lieved you'd come _ a -

long.
Hands, _____
touch - ing hands, _____

reach - ing out,
touch - ing me,
touch - ing you. _____

Sweet Car - o - line, ____
I've been in - clined ____
good times nev - er seemed so
to be - lieve they nev - er

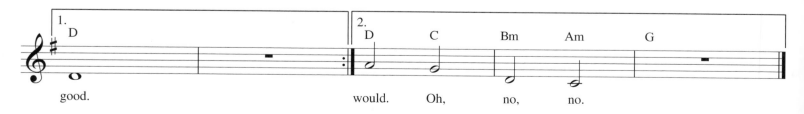

good.
would. Oh, no, no.

TILL THERE WAS YOU

from Meredith Willson's THE MUSIC MAN

TRUMPET

By MEREDITH WILLSON

THE TIMES THEY ARE A-CHANGIN'

TRUMPET

Words and Music by
BOB DYLAN

UNCHAINED MELODY

TRUMPET

Lyric by HY ZARET
Music by ALEX NORTH

TOMORROW

from The Musical Production ANNIE

TRUMPET

Lyric by MARTIN CHARNIN
Music by CHARLES STROUSE

Moderately fast

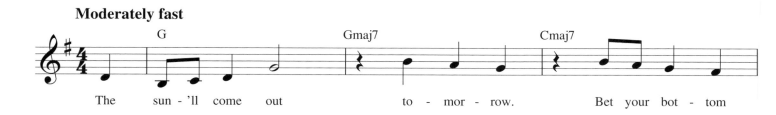

The sun-'ll come out to-mor-row. Bet your bot-tom

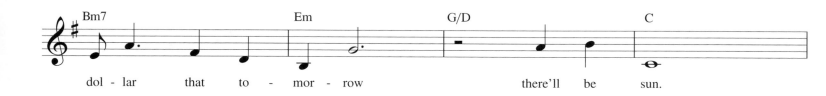

dol-lar that to-mor-row there'll be sun.

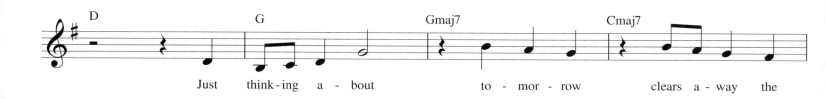

Just think-ing a-bout to-mor-row clears a-way the

cob-webs and the sor-row till there's none.

When I'm stuck with a day that's gray and lone-ly,

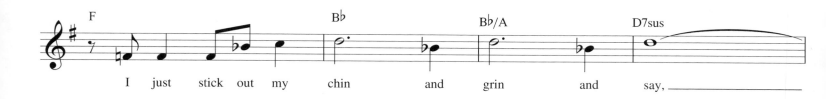

I just stick out my chin and grin and say, ___

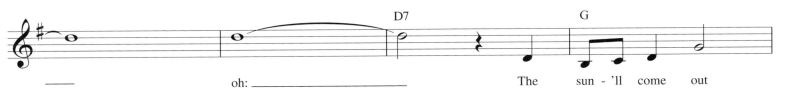

oh: _____ The sun - 'll come out

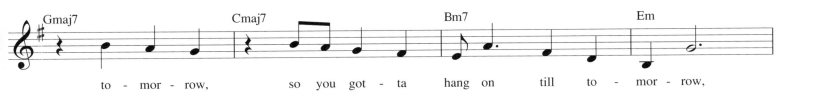

to - mor - row, so you got - ta hang on till to - mor - row,

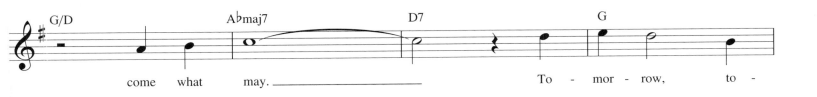

come what may. _____ To - mor - row, to -

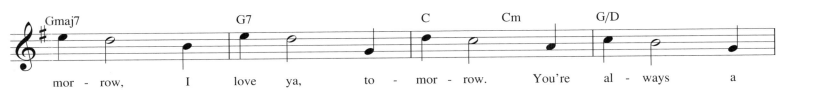

mor - row, I love ya, to - mor - row. You're al - ways a

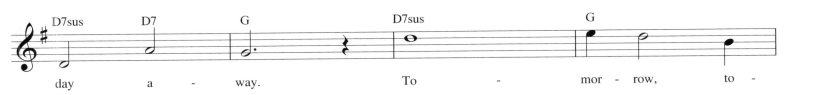

day a - way. To - mor - row, to -

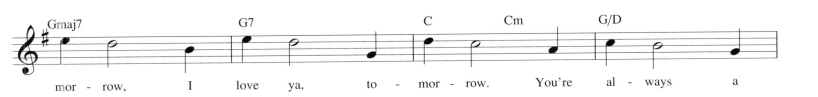

mor - row, I love ya, to - mor - row. You're al - ways a

day _____ a - way! _____

VIVA LA VIDA

TRUMPET

Words and Music by GUY BERRYMAN,
JON BUCKLAND, WILL CHAMPION
and CHRIS MARTIN

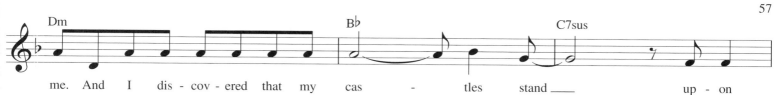

me. And I dis - cov - ered that my cas - tles stand _____ up - on

pil - lars of salt _____ and pil - lars of sand. _____ I hear Je - ru - sa - lem bells _____

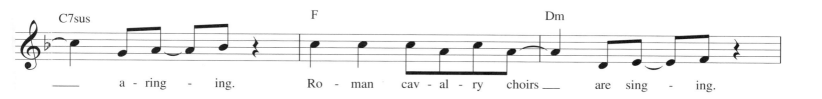

_____ a - ring - ing. Ro - man cav - al - ry choirs _____ are sing - ing.

Be my mir - ror, my sword _____ and shield, _____ my mis - sion - ar - ies in a for -

- eign field. _____ For some rea - son I can't _____ ex - plain, _____

once you've gone there was nev - er, nev - er an hon - est word, _____

_____ and that was when I ruled the world. _____

WE ARE THE WORLD

TRUMPET

Words and Music by LIONEL RICHIE
and MICHAEL JACKSON

WHAT A WONDERFUL WORLD

TRUMPET

Words and Music by GEORGE DAVID WEISS
and BOB THIELE

WONDERWALL

TRUMPET

Words and Music by
NOEL GALLAGHER

the lights _ that lead ___ us there _ are blind - ing.

There are man - y things ___ that I _____ would like to say to you, _

___ but I don't know how. _____

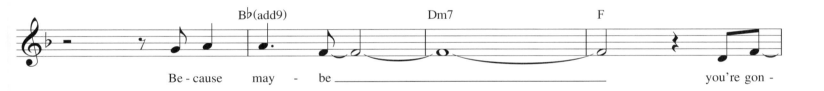

Be - cause may - be _____ you're gon -

- na be the one that saves me, _____ and

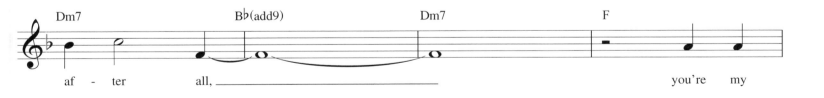

af - ter all, _____ you're my

won - der - wall. _____

YOU ARE THE SUNSHINE OF MY LIFE

TRUMPET

Words and Music by
STEVIE WONDER

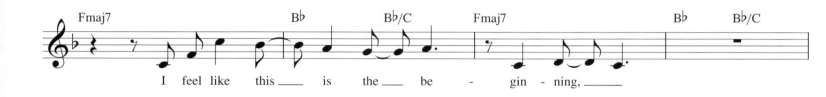

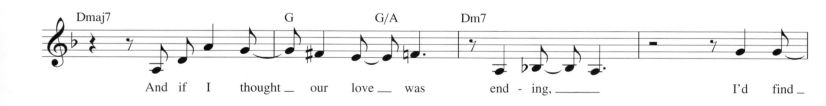

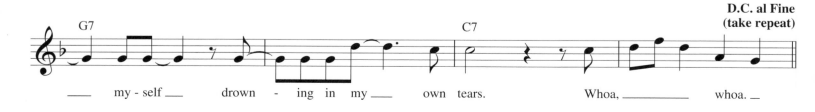

YOU'VE GOT A FRIEND

TRUMPET

Words and Music by
CAROLE KING

 Audio Access Included

HAL•LEONARD
EASY INSTRUMENTAL PLAY-ALONG

- Perfect for beginning players
- Carefully edited to include only the notes and rhythms that students learn in the first months playing their instrument
- Great-sounding demonstration and play-along tracks
- Audio tracks can be accessed online for download or streaming, using the unique code inside the book

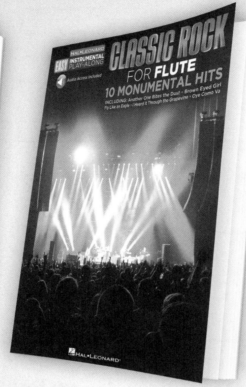

DISNEY
Book with Online Audio Tracks

The Ballad of Davy Crockett • Can You Feel the Love Tonight • Candle on the Water • I Just Can't Wait to Be King • The Medallion Calls • Mickey Mouse March • Part of Your World • Whistle While You Work • You Can Fly! You Can Fly! You Can Fly! • You'll Be in My Heart (Pop Version).

00122184	Flute	$9.99
00122185	Clarinet	$9.99
00122186	Alto Sax	$9.99
00122187	Tenor Sax	$9.99
00122188	Trumpet	$9.99
00122189	Horn	$9.99
00122190	Trombone	$9.99
00122191	Violin	$9.99
00122192	Viola	$9.99
00122193	Cello	$9.99
00122194	Keyboard Percussion	$9.99

Disney characters and artwork © Disney Enterprises, Inc.

CLASSIC ROCK
Book with Online Audio Tracks

Another One Bites the Dust • Born to Be Wild • Brown Eyed Girl • Dust in the Wind • Every Breath You Take • Fly like an Eagle • I Heard It Through the Grapevine • I Shot the Sheriff • Oye Como Va • Up Around the Bend.

00122195	Flute	$9.99
00122196	Clarinet	$9.99
00122197	Alto Sax	$9.99
00122198	Tenor Sax	$9.99
00122201	Trumpet	$9.99
00122202	Horn	$9.99
00122203	Trombone	$9.99
00122205	Violin	$9.99
00122206	Viola	$9.99
00122207	Cello	$9.99
00122208	Keyboard Percussion	$9.99

CLASSICAL THEMES
Book with Online Audio Tracks

Can Can • Carnival of Venice • Finlandia • Largo from Symphony No. 9 ("New World") • Morning • Musette in D Major • Ode to Joy • Spring • Symphony No. 1 in C Minor, Fourth Movement Excerpt • Trumpet Voluntary.

00123108	Flute	$9.99
00123109	Clarinet	$9.99
00123110	Alto Sax	$9.99
00123111	Tenor Sax	$9.99
00123112	Trumpet	$9.99
00123113	Horn	$9.99
00123114	Trombone	$9.99
00123115	Violin	$9.99
00123116	Viola	$9.99
00123117	Cello	$9.99
00123118	Keyboard Percussion	$9.99

HAL•LEONARD® CORPORATION
7777 W. BLUEMOUND RD. P.O. BOX 13819 MILWAUKEE, WI 53213
www.halleonard.com

Prices, content, and availability subject to change without notice.